I0092707

Kingdom of Glass & Seed

Jules Jacob

LILY POETRY REVIEW BOOKS

Praise for Jules Jacob

In *Kingdom of Glass & Seed,* Jules Jacob writes with an attentive eye to the smallest details of flesh and flower: "treasures where others see / nothing unusual." These poems enter the dislocated world of foster care and addiction in language that is deeply attuned to the rawness of experience, where nature is both haven and metaphor. "All mothers can be as happy / as their troubled child" writes Jacob in a collection that seeks forgiveness not retribution, that holds suffering in a tender, but alert gaze.

—Jessica Cuello, author of *Liar* and *Yours, Creature*

Copyright © 2023 by Jules Jacob
Published by Lily Poetry Review Books
223 Winter Street
Whitman, MA 02382

https://lilypoetryreview.blog/

ISBN: 978-1-957755-23-6

All rights reserved. Published in the United States by Lily Poetry Review Books.
Library of Congress Control Number: 2023938694

Cover design: Martha McCollough

For my family, especially family members who are adopted and/or lived in foster care, a group home or an orphanage.

Table of Contents

Next I dream the love is made of glass

— Anne Sexton "The Break Away"

I

Strange Birds

The bluebird that fell down my throat
        I knew well. Bathed in rainlight,

he trilled our names, winter's dormant
        grass and seed our bed to witness

sunset's attempt to mirror his coughed-out
        feathers. Bluebird knew the magpie

that absconded with his laughter.
        We choked on an ordinary Sunday.

My Mother Eats Wyoming

When asked why she loved Gillette's
Depression era soil, Mom says she can't
remember specifics other than she prized
the taste. I sweet talk, but can't persuade
her five-year-old self to appear, the one
who with her first cousins kept grasshoppers
in matchbox beds while they recovered
from amputations guaranteeing
the patients couldn't escape. Mom's
endearingly thirsty. She locates fountains
and perceives softness quickly, prefers
water hard, naïve to her divining.

Quiet Kingdom

Down ground deep
mycelium carry signals—

    maple leaves her sugars on
    too long

        oak's falling acorns
are too green to root

willow's fixated on drought.

Ash sends messages
via filigreed species

    of every little splendor
    that lives come Spring.

        Mole and man tunnel
earth, heedless of tubular

filaments communing.

Beautiful Boy, Available in Rosewood

Women knew and girls knew   old ladies
sowing cucumber seeds in their gardens knew,
your cheekbones alone could make them lie down
on a pine-needle carpet. Sawdust couldn't penetrate
your lashes   the Caribbean swam to your eyes,
sunned in honey locust skin overlaid with rosewood.
Your sixteen-year-old babysitter wouldn't stop
smoothing her hands over your bones and organs
when you were eleven. At fifteen, I knew
your white linen shirt   your strong tongue.
I hid God in the tree-canopy lace   examined
the worth of my blood, your quickmoan
and roll-off, the smell of semen, resin's faithfulness
to my shorts and your nonchalant walk home.

Rogue Waves

What weighs more heavily on the belt,
sadnesses or memories?
      —*The Book of Questions XLV,* Pablo Neruda

I remember when I managed water
as a lifeguard and body surfer,

when I sank in the deep end
to play a drowning victim.

Like a seabird, I held my breath
for minutes and attacked my rescuer.

I remember the lake called Half
Moon Pond I swam across

on a funny dare in New Hampshire,
and the soughing stand of Quaking

Aspen beside Lake Dillon
in Colorado— the relentless

falling leaves.
I remember yellow or its alloy

gold glinting in the sea,
floating chrysanthemums

and a body rising—
our arms twining a stretcher.

The Child Advocate: Home Visit

Years ago, dirt beat the grass beneath lawn chairs.
Empty gas cans, unfinished energy drinks, a backless swing.
Porch canting with cousins ghosting on heroin.

Inside, I can't see when my olfactory nerve
screams *run*. When a flea-ravaged Labrador
bumps my hand and I feel its tumor, when

mother and dog follow me to the children's
bedroom, empty except for a subfloor littered
with broken toys and pets' urine and feces.

In the rest of the house, black mold, a nearly
bare fridge, weeks of trash, and under the deck,
a dead armadillo. I long for my inhaler.

What breathes and doesn't is fraying. Children
unable to forget homes they won't return to.
I make note of the glass doorknobs and high ceilings.

One for André Breton

Always for the first time
the startle—

    from the dashboard
       across a bedspread

in the bathroom
    mirror   a shocker

on top of my head reflected.

Under a vine-twined
    pergola a sunlit filament

    swayed   a jumper
       and a runner—

from my hand   an eye-blink
    to the table's edge

and over.

How to Locate a Homeless Daughter

Search for vocal warmups and tongue twisters,
repeat, *the big black bug drank black blood.*
Be the big black bug that drank black blood,
antennae and tiny hairs tuned to Missouri
Case.net, six legs cycling through
litigant name searches and jail rosters.
Flail pincers when you find her caged, rest
briefly knowing she can eat and can't use.
With compound eyes see all her anguished
faces— realize you're wingless and in this
moment your exoskeleton fractured.
Say, *bug crawled upon the balcony*
in explicitly imitating her hiccupping,
while aimlessly inviting her in.

Anjezë Bojaxhiu Lends Her Eyes

Mother Teresa leads me on a 2 a.m. tour
of the ruins of Aleppo   two children

a grandmother, sitting on a rubble-covered
bed listening to a cranked-up gramophone—

dream-scramble of an AP photo
of a solitary man united to his shelled

apartment and possessions—
to his city's end or his.

※

I heard Let There Be Peace on Earth, my mother's
voice content with the faith I tried but failed to know

※

the peace that was meant to be.

※

An app reveals I type "hope" habitually.

※

I pretend Mother Teresa watches me
crush lemon thyme and sage   anointing

my temples and crown with selections
from the cosmic vending machine,

pretend she laughs when I water with
MiracleGro. Forget to call her Saint.

Broken Sonnet for Relapsing

Daughters, this song is yours,
what I can't spare us   what sinks
to the carpet keening night of stars trying
to leave this earth. Pain is the trembling
cat running to   not away, sacrificing
mirror neurons to dispel my disease.
The dark waits   searches stellar
deaths before they were known.
If found, we return   rearranged.
Please. No more lectures on boundaries.
All mothers   can be as happy
as their troubled child.
This is their love song.
Don't say   nebulae can't reappear.

2020 Offerings

I was gifted a bird I'd never seen.
Russet-gold feathers, white-specked underbelly, eyes
to the hot pepper suet   claws, the swaying cable line.

I was gifted a quick-stepped intruder.
A devotee to chain link fences who softened
the fall of a latch. Brown thrasher   I cherish

that you'll draw blood defending your own.
O leaf-tossing mimic, together we sing
a thousand songs as common.

If Only Aristotle

The female is, as it were, a mutilated male,
and the catamenia are semen, only not pure
for there is only one thing they have not
in them, the principle of soul.
                                    —Aristotle

A piece of chalk   snow-colored insect
from a cut zinnia, slip of Chinese paper —
You discover treasures where others see
nothing unusual, cell phone showing
search results for fluffy white, pretty bug.

               If you knew shoulders were helium
               and hydrogen   the universe expanding
               white-hot starlight deemed the color
               Cosmic Latte, would you believe
               stellar events were parables for the
               faithful— your four causes of nature
               matters between heaven and the land.

I erase Sherman Alexie's advice
to love the liars in this world
or live alone under Today's Menu
on the kitchen chalkboard   write,
Female and male same species.
Fairy fly and wooly aphid same
creature. Family: Aphidadae.

Praise to What We're Made Of

Praise our concussed brains, cracked teeth
knit bones   arteries blocked and free
vocal cords modulating air flow—
Moms telling it on the mountain
with Mahalia Jackson, Grandfathers and Patsy
Cline's resonating lonely   crazy, so blue.

Praise our arched brows, Sister, freckled
cheeks and commanding irises   yours and little
brother's opening in Saigon in '73, his DNA
confirming eighty-three percent Filipino
ten percent Chinese   Vietnamese, well,
seven percent said we could discard the GI
Joe Father/Vietnamese Mother theory.

Praise keloid scars, blood sugar spikes
T cells   blue, soft, and dark brown
eyes, nerves firing fast twitch muscle
fibers and flinches: older brother's
when he tore his cuticles   ours when
we picked scabs prematurely and found
stardust bleeding in our hands.

The Last Kate Spade Wine Glass

All conceived endings
come to the same conclusion—

cleaning up shards,
the liminalist wakes to find

she's still holding
her devoted Siamese cat,

a decade long memoir re:
replacing kids with pets.

�;

Systemic lupus, sticky lungs
SERPINA1 gene mutation:

inherited on the long arm
of the fourteenth chromosome.

☘

faith lost in the conqueror
of all conceives an end—

porous metacarpals
cupping an intact stem.

Late July, Hwy. 160

Speeding by Spokane high school's
baseball fields, I recall my son's
strong seventh inning swing.

Missing him, I box the image
with his bubble-wrapped trophies
and drive faster than the pain.

Sixty second news flash:
eighty-seven degrees, slight
wind, attack in Kabul kills ten.

New deaths, enlisted sons—
I pop a CD mix in: "Alone,"
"Pennies from Heaven"

and Tom Petty's
"Runnin' Down a Dream."
We're goin' wherever it leads.

How to Read Patterns

Mornings, he read to her in the red chair.
Little Golden Books offering passage

to Red Riding Hood's woods and the Poky
Puppy's misadventures. Snap of the paper,

crush of Pabst cans and a litany
of baseball scores his afternoon recital.

Evenings, stepmother sprawled in the chair
drank Long Island Tea and absorbed remains

of the magic. Her biological father dozed,
unaware it was missing. Sunday, Wyoming

winds brought dust and rain, fists, and tears.
She hid behind the red chair and gaped

at small imperfections in the fabric—
like the whiskers on her biological father's

face, worn and long between the jail's bars.
Two decades later while furniture shopping

with her older lover, she realized the red
chair was perfect, the fabric, tweed.

Best Blue When Robed

In depression years, my best robes
have been blue— midnight, royal, ice.
Velour with satin trim if possible.

No hard to care for velvets or silks.
No belted ties as they easily tangle
with rage while lying down.

Zippers with embellished tassels
are sharp. Gown-length necessary
to awaken ankle bones when I widow-

walk the upstairs balcony pining
for the sunrise— or tiptoe to my desk
for BIC mechanical pencils, #2

Dear Older Brother at Age Nine

I'm immobile, holding my fractured elbow
close to my side when you give up and leave
me in the park to get Mom. You return, face
pinched with wrath masking your disappointment
that you're alone. You manage to put me
on my trike, and I steer with one hand.
You drive your bike into the back of mine
again and again until we make it home.

❀

I'm six and flat on my back, left arm
heavily casted and lifted perpendicular
to my body. You're sitting on the ledge
outside my partly open hospital window
in your Catholic school uniform, the late
afternoon sun slanting lines of light behind you.
Your chatter and grins mix with December air.
You must have been cold.

The Botanist's Daughter

Dad battles sedge grass invading blueberries.
On our hike to the back pasture, he points
to wild turkeys consuming the year's crop
to juvenile chestnuts unaware of future blight.
He pauses once to discuss five-foot ruts
logging after heavy rain scored on the forest
floor, skidders dragging mature white pines
from our woodland cathedral. We head
to a high point where my grandmother
said on clear days you could see the Atlantic.
I squint past Parker Mountain, kneel and release
the red-spotted newt. I pocket a piece of mica
and pink granite. Dad says I'm thinking
of Saunders Ledge— the ocean's too far.

Colorado Things to Do and Be

If I could run across Loveland Pass
miss hairpin turns, take drop-off leaps
and freefall dives, I'd purify my Continental

Divide from ages forty-one to four,
nodding to the east and west, to silver veins
pre-mines and Red Rocks, the amphitheater.

If I could, I'd be the glint of iron pyrite
the dart of a rainbow trout or a signal arm
lowering for vanishing campfire songs.

Let me be the pine beetle's extinction
and crunch of rock candy breaking
the silence of a six-year-old left alone.

Flight Behavior Along the I-44 Corridor

Her pimp called her Birdie after paper cranes
she made from fast food napkins—
mom showed her how to fold them when she
was ten   Birdie wrote her real name on floppy
wings, left her tocsins in truck stop restrooms.
I want to say that's how she was found.
Blue jay to a nest in ropey ivy vines.
I want to say her name is Olivia Quinn
Woods, one I handpicked for resilient girls.
Red flasher to a hickory   cardinal to mate.
I need to proclaim origami saved her,
but some species and lies won't fly.

If I Were Drowning

...feel it coming in the air tonight

I   feel it   tonight   Lord
          waiting for
it
          oh Lord

          you told me you
would not
before
But
I was there and   what you did
          with my   eyes
          you can   grin,
          you've been
     all   lies

And I   feel it
well
I can feel
And

                         don't worry
How could I   forget,
          the first time, the last time
the hurt   show
          no stranger to you and me

feel   the air tonight   Lord
                    this moment

I feel it

       coming   tonight   Lord

my   life

       oh

       my life. *

* This is an erasure of the lyrics to "In the Air Tonight," written by Phil Collins

The Limnologist's Song

My granddaughter maps bacteria
in fatigued streams, sings *my constant*

friend to tide pools and freshwater bayous,
I know, I know when her booted feet

plunder mud-choked springs.
She serenades Lake Winnipesaukee,

why should I feel discouraged?
when she spots black rain,

because I'm happy swimming
to a plastic, magnetic letter Q

and *why should my heart be lonely*
as she weds it to her ring finger.

Before diving through algae blooms,
Oh, oh-oh because I'm free.

* His Eye Is on the Sparrow lyrics
  (italicized) by Civilla Durfee Martin

The Seventeenth of May

The MRI report arrives at 9:30 a.m.
We read your diagnoses before the doctor
calls and we have a chance to wish
our daughter, Happy Birthday.

One description includes "lymph node
architecture by ribbons and nests of tumor cells"
I Google *ribbon cells in metastatic lymph node.*
Results display an array of cute ribbons for sale

in colors linked to a stunning selection of cancers.
I don't know which one to poke through my lip
to announce my husband's squamous cell
carcinoma, not skin—easy to be fooled, yes—

but a primary head, neck or lung malignancy,
maybe mouth or throat, matching color
burgundy and white, or just white. Better
than grey, a coldhearted choice for the brain.

Friday the thirteenth of May is my husband's
biopsy and birthday of my biological father,
who died from complications of throat cancer.
Some coincidences are best neglected.

Retrospective on Seedlings

I battle wild violets in the vegetable beds,
        fertilize their hybrid cousins'
      'Sherry' and 'Adonis' in window boxes.

Acorns carelessly blown from the deck
        last fall, tap deep into worm castings,
      daring to toast a shoot—to light—this spring.

Saplings are dug up, tossed in trash bins.
        Eight-foot oaks in buckets are picked
      out of a lineup at local nurseries.

Theories of Late Medieval Botanists

Dr. Serban, expert in pulmonary
diseases, tells me to picture my lungs
as an upside-down tree   windpipe
the trunk, bronchial tubes branches,
air sacs called alveoli—
the leaves and blooms.
Anthracnose and ash come to mind.

※

Medieval botanists believed God
designed pulmonaria's leaves
to resemble diseased lungs
to show the illiterate their proper
usage   unaware the white
spots hid air pockets cooling
the plant they called lungwort.

※

My favorite cultivar, 'Dark Vader'
has persisted for a decade.
I adore the tiny yellow centers
and delicate pink and violet blossoms
that chameleon to blue as they age,
making them ideal for miniature
vases, but short-lived.

Battlefield Road, Summertime

Lying by the median, the Seal Point
Siamese cat's fawn-colored fur ruffled.
Was it wind produced by rush hour traffic?
When we lived in the Mark Twain National
Forest, my husband called me One Who Sees
Animals for the times I named the presence
of deer, fox, rabbits, hawks—once
a tarantula—before they appeared.
But in this city, dozens cross each day.
There's a no U-turn sign at the stoplight, no
breakdown lane. I could park on a side street,
dodge cars, clutch the dying cat   dart back.
A man in a red van keeps honking.
I signal left on South Lone Pine.

II.

Midwestern Horses Needed

He towers in coral, red
and blue   bold as any man

living on the edge
of a Thomas Hart Benton

landscape   his shadow
falling over my rolling-eyed

horse and defeated cornstalks
smoldering in charcoal slashes.

Face hidden under a hat,
shoulders bulging

and hammer in oversized
hands   he swings,

splitting the mocking
green sky and screech

of a missile before
it destroys the land.

It's All Sugar Anyway

Our favorite heirloom tomato,
a Japanese Trifele—pear-shaped
red and mahogany fruit

with green shoulders, sublime
flavor and a hint of chocolate—

softens   splits open
in the Portuguese bowl.

Tiny survivors of the Orkin
man march an alert
up the microwave   over

corn flowers circling
the porcelain rim.

Fruit flies dive slow mo
in and out and in
a pool of plum colored

syrup   oblivious
to their sweet drowning.

In Which I Roll into the Quicksilver Sea

A house I cannot place
commanded tides

from its cliff throne
and so did you when you

crashed your fist
through the sliding glass

door, leaving drops of blood
sparkling on the floor.

Cellar of Ports and Cannulas

The eighth week at the ambulatory infusion
center I'm deliberately an hour late.

I tell the receptionist I'll skip this visit
but she calls the charge manager who proclaims

send her down as if I landed on spin again
and won lifelong treatment.

Twitchy nurse Brittney states my medication
isn't ready because it can't be mixed until I

arrive— *It's exorbitantly expensive. If you
don't make it, we don't want to waste it.*

※

The following week I dress for chills
with silk under armor and Smartwool socks.

I pick a corner bay with a view
of citizens detecting ways in and out

of this cellar of ports and cannulas.
Three of my roommates are wheeled in.

Two men are out-of-it.
A young woman chokes. Coughs? Chokes.

Her husband is fetched from waiting.
My urge to bolt is full-bore-anxiety

revival of an actress ripping out her I.V.
yelling, *who the hell are these sick people?*

✻

The thirteenth week I report a minor issue,
entertaining staff with pictures of an intricate rash

identical to the lace on the back of my nightgown.
My nurse says *overactive histamine reaction.*

Charge nurse, *dermatographism!*
Ultrasound Tech, *the slightest pressure*

can generate hives. I nod.
(Brittney's skittery glance.)

When I'm having rash issues, I say, I can write
your name on my breastbone with a finger.

Looking for Little Niagara Falls

Little Niagara Falls, Strafford County
New Hampshire, United States, Unconfirmed.
This waterfall is known to exist but its stature
and/or location have not yet been verified.
    —WWD World Waterfall Database

※

I skip the turn to Pitman Road, one lizard
  brain eye on the silver truck ahead, the other
    spotting an oak too close to the blacktop—

a quick twist of the wheel would be so easy—
  but the sight of tiger lilies propagating in soil
    enriched with ancestors' bones deters me.

I ditch the lilies and wild violets fill
  the pickup's bed, the bluest racing to greeting
    card poems chiming in my head.

Dust from Barn Door Gap lays bas-relief
  streaks on my pollen coated hood,
    afternoon shadows from Blue Job Mountain

conceal the access to the old fire road,
  the gas-pump-shaped light *Warns!*
    The fly has landed on the dashboard.

I steer with my left knee—
  a skill acquired from my older brother.
    My hands slap eighty miles an hour.

Letter From My Older Brother

Dear Jules,

Your left arm cast free, skin peeling, and oddly white,
we're walking home when a green car pulls to the curb,
the front passenger door swinging open. A stout man
leans across the seat, smiling. *Come see my puppies.*
You run towards the car, and I scream, *no, no*
with such fury it startles the man, who speeds away.
Just two houses from our apartment, we step out
of the deepening shade of the elms lining 8th Street.
Sentry still, eyes locked on his taillights.

⚘

I begged you to get up ten, or maybe twenty times
after I bounced you off the high end of the teeter-
totter, your elbow first to greet the concrete.
You said, *I can't, I can't*— still as the time
you fell on the radiator and had a concussion,
as the time you fell down a set of cement steps
and a nail pierced your upper lip, as the moment
we saw the shrunken heads in an exhibit at Montréal's
World's Fair, your face whiter than your cast free arm.

Kingdom of Possibilities

for Margaret Boyle

Beyond the docile yard we stroll
past dappled shade and Callicarpa
Americana— magenta berries
gentled from outer wraps

by white tailed deer a match
to her silk dress brushing my left
knee, her hand cupping mine
gloved in glycerin and rosewater.

Each gleam from her aquamarine
earrings a hosanna, each dogtooth
violet matching its rainbow trout
leaves to the forest floor, ours.

Reclamation

Hands-clasped prayers, greed
naivety, fervency   /lit & laid

on fallow ground
for revival-green conversion.

    Saplings, roots   fungi
      slashed or burned

             sparks   away
             fritillaries   away

     larks' beaks   /open
    to claim last songs.

Ashes coat exhausted terrain
pinegrass seeds   /seek an out

rain drenches / water-runs-thru
charred cells & cyanide slurry.

Counting the Weeper's Rings

Swaying in tree pose
I breathe-in   realign
bend to chronic thirst

skip warrior III   exhaling
stronger children in eucalyptus
and Western red cedar,

hiding them in willow
hair before we drop
to corpse pose.

3 23

rain bent daffodils
muddy soles imprinting floors
spring's dirty secrets

House of Seeds & Wounds

You punctured my vein and feigned surprise
when my blood ran forsythia yellow, leaving
Rorschach blots on your favorite Italian suit.
(I saw a glass shatter into a thousand seeds breaking free.)

You watched my Larkspur eyes and cried.
You kicked the dog for my reaction.
And me without scent or color,
hidden from other pollinators.

Sometimes the Messengers Die

Praise *the dark octopus that darkened the day's peace*, *
draping arms of bad news over the maple tree.
Praise the rose breasted grosbeaks, white as printer
paper, black blacker than the octopi, piercing its flesh

with beaks bobbing precisely as sewing machines.
Praise the eight that flew straight to the cephalopod's
eyes, pecking corneas of fresh cylinders
of safflower seeds in the harshest winter.

Praise clear blood flensing ducts, pouring
down branches split like decayed bamboo,
the messenger's tears pooling by the peonies
for sandhill cranes and green head mallards.

Praise, too, the floating flock rising together
with mourning doves and red-tailed hawks
to carry us to burning rainforests in Costa Rica,
his heavy body dropping faster than mine.

* LII The Book of Questions, Pablo Neruda

The Usefulness of Carets

When I first gasped air, my grandfather quit drinking.
^ Forty years later he drank a Coors Light at a holiday gathering.

My biological father left cocaine behind in the '90s, me in the late '60's.
^ Addicts burn cash and kids like kindling.

A full bottle of Smirnoff disappeared in his truck the day of his funeral.
^ Rehab fantasies cooling, the shaman disappeared with the fix.

A drug addiction counselor said asking my daughter to stop
using (opioids) was asking an amputee to *walk* across a room.
^ Sub *skip* for (heroin) and *pirouette* for (meth).

This could be a ruse and their magic's still thriving.
^ If promoted widely, some myths come true.

88 Elm Street

Neighbors talk behind their hands,
wind bending sounds and floating bits
of fabricated concern to 88 Elm Street.

Gapkids girl soldier-stiff, her little
brother clinging to their mother, leaving
red marks of objection on her neck.

Social worker glides on twilight humidity,
murmurs to mother who folds in half neatly,
sinking with the heat stressed leaves of June.

Her tears stream black. Her dying
rabbit cries jolt her next-door neighbor's
hyper vigilant nervous system.

After the children are gone, she sits
on the juice-stained couch staring at the spot
where the T.V. promoted a better life

before it was pawned. Sweating, shaking,
withdrawing alone, she can't eat, drink
or stub out her cigarette before it burns.

To Be Called Eden

is to be ~~perfect~~ pure ~~paradise.~~
A place of ~~pristine~~ beauty

where you preside over bumble-
bee ~~funerals~~ ceremonies

and ~~extinct~~ Hawaiian honeycreepers
sing ever lingering tunes

for your thirteenth birthday.

To be called Eden is to reside
in Utopia   a state of great

~~happiness~~ endurance
where you spin on sharp

blades on fresh ice and play
your viola to liberate

neglect and irony.

Recycling the Life of Pi

Under a benzodiazepine tarp
in a boat docked on fescue
they review Mother Memories

Foster Dad screams *high*
FD gives notice, calls PO

Brother dives deep, hits
inpatient psych again

Sister rewrites the life of Pi—

Brother dies
without Mother

Sister turns into Tiger

who devours flowers

with pleasant-shaped leaves
and white petals that turn
clear as glass when it rains—

Police arrive, demand kids'
names. I offer three—
Diphylleia grayi for purists

who desire genus and species,
for consumers, Asian umbrella
leaf. Most befitting this cycle

skeleton flowers
for the translucent

who've mastered
the art of disappearing.

Land of Collective Misunderstandings

I wheel soil from a stranger's yard.
Steal clover to lure bees. Search online
for mason jars and an apiarist willing
to travel more than fifty miles away.
I want chemical-free land
but there's invasive wisteria
and wintercreeper in the yard,
Roundup in the garage.
I study consumer reports about cereals
and snack bars tainted with glyphosate,
pour Honey Nut Cheerios
into my granddaughters' bowls.

Reverie of the L-Shaped Couch

for Aiden

He's on his side on the long arm, watching
me sort through a bag of plastic party-
favor rings with interchangeable parts—
lizards, cats, moons. He reaches over, pours
the lot on the cushions and picks a green
lightning bolt. I select a purple circle
and we pop shapes together until our fingers
glitter with promise. A thin sheet of white
Styrofoam clenched between porcelain
plates in the attic escapes and floats to him.
He molds a 12 x 12-inch square to his face
before pressing it to mine. I trace his lips
and cheeks to catch his expression.
The wrench is fierce when it's gone.

Poem for a Misguided Classical Pianist

All Saints Day November 1, 2001 /
Gas station witnesses reported you filled
a 2.5-gallon plastic gas can, flicked
a lighter, shouted *I am the devil /
responsible for 9-11* through the whoosh
of flames / your screams and silence surely
prayers for martyrdom / The Houston Chronicle
asked for help identifying a victim / Months
later DNA replied, Marguerite Jacob, born
on Bastille Day / called for the last time
in September on her brother's birthday /
said *the music's gone / I sold the piano /*
March 2002, we spread your ashes in your
favorite state park, Angel / Mount Diablo.

Note to Parents

To bio fathers who disappeared,
your children are not tattoos.

Why ink their names on your bodies
when you already forgot them.

To beautiful, imperfect mothers unable
to protect their children while providing

food and shelter, forgive your mothers.
Children, forgive me.

Reseeding

Hope finds the open window
the break-crack-rift.
She drifts into addicts
and immigrants
innocents and illusionists
the lucid and insane.

She weaves around
anxiety-worry-fear
to plant assorted
cultivars— forgiveness
new job-new toy-good deed,
any variety she needs

for a pope or prisoner
CEO or pauper
coddled child
or runaway
to wake from their nightmares
and rise in the morning.

2 16

breaking winter soil
pointing new tips at me
narcissus shoots

A Way Back ~~Home~~

I fell off the earth

and cartwheeled
    through the Milky Way, damning

Sir Isaac Newton for a misstep
in his hypothesis on gravity.

      Michelangelo's angel and Rodin's
    Cupid and Psyche tumbled beside

me in newly arrived meteor showers,
spitting odds and ends of space debris.

        ❦

I asked for God.

Buddha smiled, Gandhi
    nodded and Sam Clemens

answered, *here I am.*
I plucked out tomorrows

    on Einstein's violin

and Mother Teresa pressed a cool
linen cloth to my hand—

    for the final record
    of your countenance, she said.

        ❦

Mark Twain winked,

wrote *dash-30-dash* and *safe passage*
before snatching the telescope

from Hubble's hand. Mark said,
look through here, dear, it's your

new *Big Bang Beginning—*
in thirteen billion years,

we'll know if you fell
to earth again.

Before the Fly Settles

And she lets the river answer
                    —Leonard Cohen

When I question the river, a chorus
of invisible frogs trills *where, where.*
When I let the river answer, she sets
a baritone soloist in the tall still weeds
behind me. *There*, familial home, gliding
trails of kayaks, siblings, father. *Air,*
air, I plead. Waves slap the concrete
boat path. Wind breathes my will,
bends my way. Her hair shiny brown
in September light and wet to her knees,
my mother casts her line back before
introducing her nymph to the water.

How to Walk in the Rain

for Richard

We'll be on MythBusters, cameramen
clomping by sea grass and rose hips,

gulls waved away, their lenses snaking
the line of the Atlantic meeting sand.

We'll discuss our favorite episode,
Walking Versus Running in the Rain.

You, walking steadily. Me running, jumping
puddles. (Turned out slower equaled dryer.)

The producer will stand on the Old Orchard Beach
pier, your mom backstroking from the horizon.

She'll speak Portuguese, serve 1950s
Sao Paulo with a kick of gin at 9,000

feet in the Rockies, the salted
air crisped by juniper and cabasas.

We'll prove time loops backwards,
current actions changing the past.

You'll toast the hours. I'll break
our glasses, set the year forward.

Acknowledgements

Grateful acknowledgment is made to the editors of the following publications in which these poems, some in earlier versions or with different titles, first appeared:

"Late July, Hwy. 160" and "Reseeding": *Camroc Press Review*
"If Only Aristotle": *Glass: A Journal of Poetry*
"In Which I Roll into the Quicksilver Sea" and "Jellyfish Dance":
    Grey Sparrow Journal
"Reclamation": *Hare's Paw Literary Review*
"How to Read Patterns," "House of Seeds & Wounds," "88 Elm St.,"
and "A Way Back Home": *The Glass Sponge,* Finishing Line Press
"The Limnologist's Song": *Lily Poetry Review*
"Rogue Waves": *Lines + Stars*
"How to Locate A Homeless Daughter": *Mid/South Sonnets: A Belle*
    Point Press Anthology
"Before the Fly Settles," "Broken Sonnet for Relapsing," and
    "Land of Collective Misunderstandings": *Mom Egg Review*
"Beautiful Boy, Available in Rosewood": *Paper Nautilus*
"How to Walk in the Rain": *Pittsburgh Poetry Review*
"One for André Breton": *Plume Poetry*
"My Mother Eats Wyoming": *Plume Poetry 8*
"If I Were Drowning," "Letter From My Older Brother," and "Praise
    to What We're Of": *Rust + Moth*
"2020 Offerings," "Before the Fly Settles," and "Counting the Weeper's
    Rings": *SWWIM*
"Strange Birds": *Third Wednesday*
"Best Blue When Robed" and "The Child Advocate: Home Visit":
    The Tishman Review
"Anjezë Bojaxhiu Lends Her Eyes": *Watershed Review*
"Battlefield Road, Summertime": *The Westchester Review*
"Flight Behavior Along the I-44 Corridor": *West Trestle Review*
"Midwestern Horses Needed": *Yes Poetry*

Special appreciation to the following writers, teachers, editors, publishers, and writing centers for showing interest in my work:

Eileen Cleary, founder and Editor-in-Chief of *Lily Poetry Review* and Lily Poetry Review books; Dr. Marilyn Kallet, Knoxville Poet Laureate and Professor Emerita of English at the University of Tennessee; The Virginia Center for the Creative Arts, Moulin à Nef France; Daniel Lawless, Editor of *Plume Poetry;* Roberta Pitman, mother and English instructor; Kenneth Pitman, father and science instructor; Dr. Harrison Solow, Eschatologist, Writer, Speaker and Pushcart Prize winner; Huntington Sharp, former Senior Editor of Red Room; The Hudson Valley Writers Center, and Finishing Line Press for selecting "The Glass Sponge" chapbook as a semi-finalist in the New Women's Voices Series where the following poems first appeared: "88 Elm Street," "House of Seeds & Wounds," "How to Read Patterns," and "A Way Back Home."

About the Author

Jules Jacob is the author of *The Glass Sponge,* a semi-finalist in The New Women's Voices Series (Finishing Line Press), and co-author with Sonja Johanson of the illustrated chapbook, *Rappaccini's Garden* (White Stag Publishing, December 2023). Her poems are featured in journals and anthologies including *Plume, Rust + Moth, Lily Poetry Review, The Westchester Review, Mid/South Sonnets, MER,* and elsewhere. Jules is an Emeritus Master Gardener, recipient of a fellowship from the Virginia Center for the Creative Arts in Auvillar, France, and former Court Appointed Special Advocate for the Thirty-first Circuit Court of Missouri.

www.ingramcontent.com/pod-product-compliance
Lightning Source LLC
Chambersburg PA
CBHW022105020426
42335CB00012B/838